PRETEND THE BALL IS NAMED JIM CROW

PRETEND THE BALL
IS NAMED
JIM CROW

THE STORY OF JOSH GIBSON

Poems by
DORIAN HAIRSTON

UNIVERSITY PRESS OF KENTUCKY

A note to the reader: This volume includes racial slurs and other sensitive language for the purpose of historical accuracy. Discretion is advised.

Editorial and Sales Offices: The University Press of Kentucky
663 South Limestone Street, Lexington, Kentucky 40508-4008
www.kentuckypress.com

Library of Congress Cataloging-in-Publication Data

Names: Hairston, Dorian, author.
Title: Pretend the ball is named Jim Crow : the story of Josh Gibson / poems by Dorian Hairston.
Description: Lexington : The University Press of Kentucky, 2024.
Identifiers: LCCN 2023040800 (print) | LCCN 2023040801 (ebook) | ISBN 9780813198873 (cloth) | ISBN 9780813198880 (paperback) | ISBN 9780813198903 (adobe pdf) | ISBN 9780813198897 (epub)
Subjects: LCSH: Gibson, Josh, 1911–1947—Poetry. | Social problems—Poetry. | Baseball—Poetry. | African Americans—History—Poetry. | LCGFT: Biographical poetry. | Poetry.
Classification: LCC PS3608.A545345 P74 2024 (print) | LCC PS3608.A545345 (ebook) | DDC 811/.6—dc23/eng/20230915
LC record available at https://lccn.loc.gov/2023040800
LC ebook record available at https://lccn.loc.gov/2023040801

Member of the Association
of University Presses

For Mom, Dad, Devin, Reecie, Amiri, and Damian

CONTENTS

Extra Innings

AUTHOR'S NOTE

Joshua "Josh" Gibson is the greatest catcher to ever play the game of baseball. Any list that does not place him at the top among field generals and among the greatest position players of all time is incomplete. In his career, Josh likely hit upwards of eight hundred home runs, and Happy Chandler, the commissioner of baseball during its integration, said Josh was the greatest catcher he ever saw. Baseball, much like the country that birthed it, has always had two lists of the most exceptional, the brightest, the fastest, the strongest, et cetera. One list is spoken and understood by all to include the full spectrum of folks who have contributed to the lore of the game. The other is written down, and though in black ink, it leaves out anything Black. This is just one of the many injustices in this story, and by no means the most painful.

Josh was born in Buena Vista, Georgia, in December 1911 and died on January 20, 1947, just a few months before Jackie Robinson broke Major League Baseball's de facto color barrier in April. He met his wife, Helen Mason Gibson, in 1928, and they married in '29. The couple had a set of twins in 1930, and Helen tragically died delivering them. Their only children would bear their parents' names (Josh and Helen Gibson), and Josh Jr. would go on to have a short career in the Negro Leagues.

Each member of this family's voice is represented here through persona poems. Some of the other voices that you will hear include those of Hooks Tinker, who is often credited with discovering Josh Gibson and for offering some sobering insight into the trauma he was exposed to and forced to endure. Chester Washington, a journalist and sports editor for the *Pittsburgh Courier,* followed much of Josh's stint with the Homestead Grays and the Pittsburgh Crawfords. Had it not been for Major League Baseball's refusal to allow Black players to join the league, the Cy Young Award would likely have been named for Satchel Paige.

Baseball is one of few sports with arbitrary yet clearly defined unwritten rules. These are defined by culture, class, race, gender norms, and a whole host of other markers that those who make the rules seldom even acknowledge had any influence on the rules, which must never be broken (until they are). This aspect of the game was the rebar to its color barrier. Additionally, this is the bedrock of baseball's slow and incomplete acceptance of the many cultures that have grown to love it. One of the most beautiful aspects of the game, however, is its capacity for change and its ability to lead America on a similar path.

Baseball history, much like the history of this country, is often the story of a bunch of fascinating truths that a minority tries to cover with some rather boring lies. This collection aims to explore the effort and lengths folks go through to uphold those lies. But I mention this point especially to highlight that the stories we tell ourselves about our past are far less interesting than the truth. America spent, or is spending—depending on the day of the week— centuries denying its own citizens the liberties they created with their labor, blood, tears, and love. Baseball's story is the same. At every rounding of the base, in every lace on the seams of the ball, in every grain of the bat, baseball holds all of America, even when it tries to shut out entire races of people. Baseball's survival, its glory, and its ability to activate the specific nostalgia that is uniquely ours rests in the hands of every person who has ever held a bat, and any attempt to rob us of that joy is futile.

In the locker room at the University of Kentucky, my baseball coach, Gary Henderson, posted a quote from Negro League and Giants great Willie Mays: "Baseball is a game, yes. It is also a business. But what it most truly is is disguised combat. For all its gentility, its almost leisurely pace, baseball is violence under wraps."

Baseball is harsh enough without adding all the race nonsense that owners were so preoccupied with until and beyond Jackie Robinson's 1947 Rookie of the Year performance. The players of the 1920s–1940s understood one thing: competition. Those who were true competitors during Major League Baseball's darkest hours, players from the Negro Leagues and MLB teams, would barnstorm across America playing each other in integrated baseball games that showed everyone who the best really was. According to Dizzy Dean, the only thing keeping the Cardinals from a perpetual pennant run was the front office's stubbornness in not hiring the talent in the Negro Leagues, specifically Satchel Paige and Josh Gibson.

As an institution, the Negro Leagues provided jobs for an entire community that could not—or would at least struggle to—otherwise gain legal employment. They provided entertainment and opportunity to a people that had been subjugated and oppressed in their every attempt to be happy and free. Negro League baseball was the best the sport had to offer. What I am constantly amazed by in the leagues' history is their refusal to discriminate. Moreover, I have fallen in love with the way they welcomed creativity, style, flair, showmanship, grace, and most importantly, how the only requirement was that you show up to the field able to play.

Josh never played an inning of "organized" or "official" baseball. All the other parts of him, as a Black man, would have made him too human—would have meant he deserved freedom. He was a widower, a husband, a father, a son, a man, a child, a lover, a fighter, a damn good baseball player, just like thousands of other folks who have felt their cleats split the freshly dug dirt before the first pitch. As you read these poems, I implore you to consider why there was a need for the Negro Leagues in the first place.

Play Ball!

BOTTOM OF THE FIRST

0–0

Manifesto for Black Baseball Players

Josh Gibson

never forget the 42 reasons
baseball is best played with color

steal bases like they
stole this country

break into record books
turn more than just they ink black

pretend the ball is named
jim crow

(de)colonize
the hall of fame

remember we gave the game
lights, helmets, and style

never be controlled
by anything white

belt "Lift Every Voice and Sing"
during they national anthem

find you a Helen drop down on one knee
place a baseball field on her fourth finger

Smuggling Strength

Josh Gibson

up here the water
of the Allegheny
and the Monongahela
bend just enough to keep
the klan at bay.

my Papa say the white man
down south done made it so
the whole family need to make
they way up north.

say Buena Vista, Georgia
with all the po folks' shacks
we made into homes ain't safe
as the protection these walls
this steel mill offer.

he told me he made good
with a conductor and got a whole train
to slither its way down the tracks
through the hills, mountains, and valleys
between the old home and the new one
to get us away from all that hate
below the Mason–Dixon
then he say the only reason
them other folk we saw on the train
got to hitch a ride was cause he nice.

when we all got as situated as we could
Papa used to say how he feel the mill ain't safe
for me. something about my ears
too young to catch any of that
grown men talk as he call it
when they splitting steel up
but by the time I was fifteen,
with the way rent, water,
food, Mama's habits, all cost
more than we got
everyone need to find work.

he ain't hold my hand
when I walked in my first day,
no introducing me to anyone.
but he did warn me how the mill
different than picking cotton
the way steel can get hotter
than if you could touch
the Georgia sun raw,
and if I ain't careful
steel got a perfect coffin
picked out for me.

by seventeen, I learned the way the whistle
blows like the rooster crows right before
sunup. I mastered the art of beating
that sound by a few minutes to sneak
myself a couple treasures before folk eyes opened.

I would tiptoe through the gate
pretend to start work early while

I'd slide some steel up under my skin
and massage it in until it replaced
every single muscle I got.

the problem I ain't never
considered is what happens
when the steel starts
to rust and it be hard as hell
to get the medicine to it?

Naming

Helen Gibson

Doc says there are two sets of feet
trying to stretch themselves a little more
room inside me, and they running out

of space. I feel they might be
searching for another belly soon
the way they wrestle each other
into a comfortable position.

it's like all the secrets and promises
Josh has blown into my ear
have slid into my womb
and grown themselves too big
for what Doc say is my too-small frame.

we both think he's wrong.

Josh's favorite thing to do when he
try to catch some sleep
is to place his callus-covered hands
on my tummy an try to guess
which part of the twins is on the
other side of my stretched-out
thin layer of skin.

as he doze off
he like to tell them how
he prays they come out looking
as good as they mom.
he even tries out a few names on them
then place his head close
to listen for the twins' approval.

we all let him play his game.

when Josh gets to sleep and snores
enough times for them to feel
confident he out for good,
the twins whisper up in my ear
exactly what they want to be called
and make me promise to keep it a secret.

Home Run #1

Dear Helen,

I snuck this one into the bucket
of game balls. Sealed the envelope
by stitching it closed with the bright
red laces from your favorite shoes.

Spent hours trying to squeeze
each second of two years into
five and a quarter ounces of white
leather wound tight around the core
of a ball. This is my first letter.

The first of many. Just one of these
can't hold all this love, so I will pretend
each ball can fly its way through
the stars to you. I'll split each message up,
ball after ball, home run after home run.
'Til god get tired of all them broken windows
up in Heaven and bring me there too.

Love,
Josh

Night Visions

Josh Jr.

Auntie say they just nightmares,
but they the realest thing I ever seen.
Papa is in some hospital room
with walls darker than he is
when he come home in the summer.

I never can tell
if the screams are me
my sister
or Papa
or Granny
or some ghost.

the doctor hold us
like little secrets
but Papa refuse
to even touch or look at
his two little mirrors
like he disgusted at the
image we spit back at him
or worse the memory
of all the dreams he used to have.

he just stare at Mama
sleeping real peaceful
right exhausted.

when the doctor try
and hand us to Papa
an echo of
I don't want them, I want my wife
takes the knees right out
from under Big Josh.

that's when I wake up.
an auntie come in
say I been screaming
wipes the sweat off my face
tells the lie, *everything is alright.*

I told Auntie once about my nightmare
an ask if it was as real as it feels
she tell me we got our names
three whole weeks
after we was born
cause it hurt Papa too much.

now, I always freeze
the nightmare when
we all in the room together
and Mama just sleep
Helen and I ain't named yet
and Papa got his family back.

Brooklyn

Hooks Tinker

after "Harlem" by Langston Hughes

What happens to a dream assimilated?

Does it splinter like a broken bat from a fastball on the hands?
Or blister like palms after too many swings?
Or rip like a tattered glove forgotten in the elements?
Does it reek like molded cleats inside rejected locker rooms?
Or is it colonized by weeds like abandoned fields?

Maybe it's just heavy like a waterlogged ball
or the number 42 stitched on every jersey each April 15th?

Or does it erode?

Uncovered

Hooks Tinker

first time I seen Josh he was sixteen
black as the bravest of them soldiers
in the Union army
strong as the backs of all the Mamas
who found a way to carry us for nine
whole months and big enough to pass
for thirty.

this youngster grabbed a small
forty-ounce tree wrapped his fingers
around the handle waved it through
the air a few times and asked how recent
the poor thing was chopped down.

he whispered a little something to the bat
right before he stepped to the plate.

I never seen something so smooth.
how Josh didn't rock or sway back
before the pitch, he just waited there
in the box like a snake to strike
with hands so fast that
from left field you
could hear the wind jump
out the way.

the ball couldn't move quick like the breeze.
found itself in a crater over five hundred
feet from home plate by the time
it finished its long flight.

most impressive was the sound.
It was like how the light splits the sky
or sometime a tree in one of them
April storms down south.

that was our first time
hearing a ball wince.
the next swing
let us know
it wasn't our last.

Dear Diary

Helen Gibson Jr.

When Papa say that he ain't got no
or ain't big on religion, he only tellin'
half the truth.

See, I understand what he really mean
is that he ain't one to get down
on his bad knee or his good one,
and most definitely not both, to pray
or worship some god that he feel took,
or at least tried to take, love away.

He say Mama did, though: believe that is.
Said she could sing, too. maybe that be
the music I hear when I get alone
and ain't got nothin' to keep me busy.

One time he let slip that she could cook, too.
Something 'bout some collards or cornbread
but he trailed off before I could ask.

And one night, it was just me and him
in the main room across from each other
and neither of us said a word. In that silence,
I just really wanted to know what it was like
you know? that first time he *knew* it was her.

And I wish I could ask him about Mama
you know? maybe not have to guess
so much or hear from her side of the family
and it ain't that I don't believe them
it's just

I think you understand.

Anyway, when Papa say
he ain't got no belief
what he really mean
is that wouldn't no one
be able to make sense
of that thing that he always chasing.

And I know him well enough
to see that he ain't just
lookin' for Mama
or running from pain
or playing a game
to mask some anger
or drinking to escape
what his life really is.

And you know it may be all that
but on some nights
when Jr. over a friend's
and it's just me
that song gets a little more clear
and I know it's Mama
and she is trying to tell me
all that Papa cain't.

Papa Tells the Truth

Josh Gibson Jr.

Papa tells me stories
about how them white folk
down in Buena Vista, Georgia
would call him boy instead
of the name he liked so much
he gave it to me too.

tell me he got called nigger
so many times he forgot
what his real name sound like
off the lips of anybody who ain't black.

say when he and Annie and Jerry and Granny
packed they bags to move up north with
Granddaddy, Daddy's suitcase had everything
but nigger inside it. just some clothes, a few snacks
and a book for electricians to learn
how to carry light cross wires.

he always say it's when they use
boy not   *nigger*
that confuse him the most. he say
they both wrong but wonder
if a boy is the best
hitter to ever play the game,
could hit a home run off any white
man in the country, could whoop
every one of them off the field

at the same time,
what's that say about them?

he always remind me
he ain't no bronzed bambino
no Black babe ruth.
he ain't nobody's nigger.
damn sure ain't no boy.

he likes to dig his pointer
finger into my chest
and some of that energy
that he spent a second studying
builds up in his finger
shoots straight deep
into my soul
and when he knows it's there
he makes me swear
to remember my only name
is Josh Gibson.

Premature

Hooks Tinker

Josh come out the womb
built like young bamboo.
shot up so quick
his body skipped
straight to a man.

he can throw a ball faster
than steam come off hot steel.
able to swing a small tree
with plenty force to make a ball
kiss the stars
before he even touch first.

he got the strength of two oxen
three babe ruths
four of the Pirates' best hitters,
and about fifteen grown men.
But he wasn't nothing but a boy.

It ain't his strength or his good
looks or his ability to burrow
inside the best hitter's head
until they look like they never
played the game in they life
that made him so bad.

the only snag with Josh
was that he grew up
too damn fast.

BOTTOM OF THE FOURTH
1–0 GRAYS

The Original Dodgers

Hooks Tinker

the traveling circus advertises
hit a nigger and win a cigar!

to them it's innocent hopscotch
it's skipping rope, it's a good coon hunt.

milton bradley calls it the
jolly darkey target game.
a wide hole with no teeth
outlined by crimson swollen lips
means the player must pretend
a black man's head pokes
through the open hole, becomes
a tar-covered tongue

a bullseye, his body festers on a stool
as balls try to split open a forehead.

Jackie Robinson was
never the first black Dodger.

we done dodged balls for centuries
rent, lynch mobs, overseers, slave catchers,
waded through fixed elections, and rivers,
done outrun horses and bloodhounds,
even dodged some bullets a few times.

but here soon we might just turn ourselves into
Josh Gibson and america will find us in a 2–0 count
standing with a straight spine
inside the batter's box
towering over the plate
waiting for they next pitch
waiting for they next mistake
and we guarantee it won't come back.

Seen It Coming (1951)

Hooks Tinker

when they came over to our fields
in they Model Ts shaped like spanish

ships, dressed in they european
suits, fat fingers gripping Cuban

cigars, they lowered their anchors,
and tied their boats to docks

of Negro League ballparks just long
enough to marvel at all they future

profit draped in baseball uniforms.
they planted their feet on African-

built shores, pulled out they
stopwatches, pens, and jotters

to measure the dollar signs they
branded on each black muscle.

this how they searched for who would
help them raise they new pennants

for cheap, or free. they picked out
their favorites, plucked at bedrock

until whole nations crumbled,
watched their walls Jericho,

raided all our resources,
gave birth to the devil,

then ripped off our eyelids
to make sure we couldn't look away.

Pregame Cut

Josh Gibson

I wish my hair grew the speed
of my bat through the zone
and make it so I need to take a trip
to my barber every morning.

it's like when them clippers first click,
buzz their way through to a new man,
we can laugh away the big boss,
the policeman that said we too dark
to be anywhere, our woman at home waiting
inside the front door, hip cocked
to one side, 'tude the shape
of an arm holding up a child,
and our other woman cross town
who makes us forget, all at the same time.

seems some energy, almost magic
hides itself in the alcohol burn, the near fights,
the real ones, the awkward way us men pretend
we don't love each other
and finds its way down deep inside
where the baseball player lives,
and demands me to walk the whole
three blocks down the street to the field.

on game days, the old man playing checkers
in the corner that no one ever sits in, pretending
the ash tray across the board is his opponent,

likes to gloat that he is undefeated.
But then he'll jive how a home run always comes
the same day I end up underneath my barber's hands
an I perk up cause he might just be right.
he likes to call me the Reverse Samson.

and I wish my hair grew fast,
that my strength came from a fresh cut,
and life was the inside of a Black Barbershop.

West Field

Hooks Tinker

some folk say Black Ball
ain't baseball
and they right.

when a man save up all week
to drop his last copper
to come see us play
it become more than a game.

when the collection plate
get passed around on Sunday
and the whole family just touch
the rim knowing they spending
the Lord's ten percent on an afternoon
at the field we understand we are forgiven.

this is one of the few times we able
to let ourselves shine to the fullest.

even white folk bring
they lunchboxes and gloves
and they dog to the park,
spend they whole afternoon
rubbing elbows,
and clapping,
and cheering
dancing with us.

I seen a man
get down on one knee,
about halfway up third baseline,
and ask his woman
to go to every
game with him
for the rest a they life.

it ain't baseball
we offer folk
when they lay down their money
to watch some Black Ball.

we offer up the one place
where we all agree
a Negro ain't nothing
but a man.

Can't Compete

Josh Gibson

some say we got too many thieves
or we too corrupt to play
ball with them white
boys but we all know
what they really mean.

they must be referring
to how Cool Papa Bell
steal second and third
on the same pitch.

how the Crawfords
and Cubans hint pitches
to they teammates
after they decipher
which fingers in the catcher's
sequence of numbers
signals which pitch is coming.

I'd bet my last copper
it's them pitchers
using cheese graters, spit,
cooking grease, razor blades, anything
that might add a little bite
to the tail end of a two-seamer
or some depth to a curveball
that cuts so sharp it disappears.

unlike them, we smart enough
to change signals
sneak in the back door
pick off anyone looking to snatch
some signs or a base.

we know how much smoke
Satch need to blow up
a batter's nose
to mark his territory.

we got enough sense to see baseball
got rules that won't ever make the books
and we mind them the same way the game
demands every real ballplayer to.

they can say that baseball different
than the real life they like to jive
their way through but deep in the black holes
of they mind and spirit they know by saying we too
corrupt or broken or mean or nasty or black

they just admitted they scared
to get they ass beat
at they own game.

Trash Talk

Josh Gibson

when I first started to catch,
I'd sit like I was in a rocking chair
and call a clean game. I'd ask batters
how they day was, make pleasant
conversation, and only let out the occasional
chuckle after a called strike three
if I didn't like the way they voice sounded
or if they was bold enough to outright ignore me altogether.

after a couple seasons with the big fellas
I grew up enough to look them in they eyes.
Felt tall enough to show them how much bigger I am.
I graduated myself from soft chatter,
got my diploma in more pleasurable
forms of shucking like the way I whisper
the wrong pitch to throw them off balance
tell the batter *bender* or *deuce* then drop
a sign for the pitcher to play a little chin music
to make them dance. then let them know
their lady friend told me how her man had two left feet
and I can't come to they defense no more.

by the time I was a seasoned vet
I learned the only thing hitters hate
more than a little white lie is when
I tell them the black truth.

I reach into the fresh memory of last night
pull out a perfect description
of they upstairs bedroom,
describe the color of the paint
on they woman's big toe in they first at-bat,
how the lampshade don't dim the lights enough
for the family picture on the nightstand to get
anything other than a front row seat
of a lot of bare glistening skin.

then by they second visit to the plate
I break down each see-through thread of that nightgown
they wife like to wear, the one he got for their anniversary
and the way it matches the old torn-up drapes hanging
over the bathroom window and how the bathtub
barely big enough for the both of us,
but if he good I'll let him watch.

by round three I map out all the
ideas I have for new ways to arrange some furniture
but make sure to slide in a note about how
if he keep playing like this
he'll have to ask me for the money for it
and mention how I know a way to get rid
of the bed squeak that almost too loud
drown her out and right before I apologize
for the hole in the wall I play like I'm sorry
that he didn't know that neither the bed
or she can make noise.

by they fourth at-bat
if they ain't take themselves
out the game yet

I start naming bedroom secrets
how her birthmark
on her inner thigh
look like one of the states
I learned about back in school
and I ask him if he can help me remember
and in long drawn out strokes of detail
I tell him the way a kiss on the back
of her shoulder blade
opens up all types of new languages
then apologize again for any bruises I left
and make sure he knows she begged for them

in all this time, no one ever been dumb enough
to even think about turning they head
to curl their lips to say anything to me.

they just swing through strike three.
drop they dignity at the plate.
and I remind them to hold tight
to they little bat as they mosey
on back to the dugout.

Bat Considers Considering a Strike

Them fellas talk real different
when it's just them in the locker room

josh and his teammates play
like their so-called sweethearts
more like cheap liquor
or something you break down
and sprinkle into the end of a pipe
than a heartbeat or a woman or both

but if you really listen,
all that talk about the only way
and place they like they women
really just some weird game they play
to measure themselves without
actually having to do so

They lucky I never choose to speak in here
cause I'd tell them all about how I was there
when they was being crafted and shaped
and nourished by and inside that black womb
and how I whispered my babies' names
into the ears of everyone in that room

how them same breast that they can't shut
they mouths 'bout done put all them muscles
on that frame they pretend is godlike

and how they waste that bronze skin on bad magic
when they speak spells like they do

They better be glad that I ain't so foolish
to spend my time bragging about four
or five minutes if I'm generous

That I spend all my energy jumping in
and out of what they call the future

Everywhere I been, they can't see past
whatever they got in they hands
and while they waste they power
shuckin' 'n' jivin' they way through
all they pain and suffering
they lack the vision to think
for one moment
how lucky they is
that in the bottom of the ninth
I never even contemplate
going on strike

Home Run #270

Dear Helen,

I ain't worried that one day
they might weigh my bat
to see if it's the source of my strength.
I just need them to focus on the how,
not the why, of all these home runs.
they can't never discover the baseballs
I smuggled into the stadium got these letters
inside. I pray they never see how the leather glows
in the dark when it gets too close to finding you,
that the pitcher never squeeze too hard
in the wrong spot, bust open the seams,
and explode this ink everywhere.

one day I will figure a way to fit myself
inside a ball. then, I can give you more
than just words.

Love,
Josh

Dear Mama

Josh Gibson Jr.

Papa got trust issues.
won't even let his own teammates
come to his side in a fight.

when I'm batboy
he hand me all his jewelry
before the game and make me promise
that if he get hurt, I lock it all up in a safe
swallow the key then sprint my way to his side.
but, I ain't allowed to ask if he all right.
he say to check his pockets first,
make sure none of them thieves
got to him just yet.

Papa funny like that. He honest, though.
maybe that's why he got a weird
way of showing love
'specially to the two of us.

I remember one time
he find out I got bullies at school
and he come turn the whole cafeteria
upside down 'til someone
showed him where they was.

he snatched those boys up
like a handful of grass to check the wind
held them by the neck

of they shirt and with
his clenched fist bigger
than both they four baseballs
he almost get as scary as Granny
when I forget a chore.

but when he grab them boys up
like he was the sheriff or someone else
with the full might of the ugly side of this country
behind him all I saw was the empty seat next to me
and I almost said something but instead
just sat down and finished my lunch.

Your Enough Ain't Enough

Hooks Tinker

If you ever been confused
about how humans
can be bought and sold
like stock
or how they can
be bred like horses
branded like cattle
whipped like beasts

If you can't see
how one
can chain another
human being
on their back
to a stranger
in the soot-black pit
of slave ships
where the ocean's
salty spit fights a war
with piss on skin

If you don't understand
how one can be
made to pick cotton
harvest rice
hang tobacco
or people
for free

lay down rails
pave roads
build countries
make wealth
for free
be wealth

if this seem foreign to you
ain't no way you can see
an american Negro soldier
like Jackie Robinson
breaking the color barrier
is nowhere near
enough progress

Not Fit for Service

Josh Gibson

they stamped 4-F
on my paperwork
say it's my knees
or I drink too much
but we all know the truth.

uncle sam knocked
on my door drafting
some black shields
for his white sons
and I answered in my draws
slung my bat up over
my shoulder and point him
in the opposite direction.

when he stopped the bus
on one of our road trips
asking me to hop
on a boat and lead
folk to freedom,
I remind him my ancestors
say we tired of outrunning
u.s. lynch mobs here and abroad.

he showed up to the field
looking for the bronzed bambino
so I used the nearest bat to help
him pronounce my name right.

when he asked me to go fight
for all his glory somewhere else
while he still hunts me here,
I drew him a flag and lady liberty
on a baseball, handed it to the opposing
pitcher, and showed everyone exactly
what I think about his army.

Pregame Prayer

Hooks Tinker

> No refuge could save the hireling and slave
> from the terror of flight or the gloom of the grave.
> —*Francis Scott Key, "The Star-Spangled Banner"*

when we first hear
oh say can you see
we always hold our breath
and pray real quiet.

ask our God to protect us
cause it seem that so-called anthem
be the opening number
for lynch mobs all over
the land of the free.

their horse's hooves be bombs bursting
on dirt roads to the first Negro
they find that they think will look good
dangling from a tree.

with they hand-held rockets on hip
they raise they torches high enough
to make they white mask bright as stars
as they repeat a favorite
bible verse below their altar
of burnt, coal-black skin
then offer up the last
of they tar and feathers.

I heard before they leave
they spectacle, before they hang
up they white robes and replace
them with black ones, substitute
castrating irons for gavels,
or camouflage white crosses
inside police badges
they recite the pledge of allegiance
to the flag that has doubled as a noose.

then men women and children
collect souvenirs like
a finger for a home run ball
or a foot as a splinted bat.

so, before every game
while they national anthem
is played, I drop down
to a knee and pray
to our God
that they god
stay the hell away
from us.

TOP OF THE FIFTH

2–2

Telegram to Pittsburgh Pirates

Chester Washington

white newspapers claim pennant needed. Stop.
Black ballplayers the answer. Stop.
Satchel Paige Pitcher. Stop.
Cool Papa Bell OF. Stop.
All Pittsburgh Crawfords. Stop.
Buck Leonard 1B. Stop.
Ray Brown Pitcher. Stop.
Josh Gibson Catcher. Stop.
All Homestead Grays. Stop.
All affordable ready to win. Stop.
Ready to prove they can play

Gator Belt

Josh Jr.

I used to practice my four-letter words
on Helen when I knew Papa
was too far away to hear them.

if he was still in the states,
I'd say them real fast
just in case he was coming by
for an unscheduled visit
to drop off some "just cuz" money.

if he was down in Puerto Rico
or somewhere in the land south
of Mexico, and especially if he was down
in the DR or Cuba, I'd let them slide out
slow and long to make sure they bite hard enough.

Granny heard one of these
an told Papa when he made his way back
from work 'bout six months later.

that woman can't remember
to cut off the oven but
after all that time can recall
'xactly how I sounded,
even matching the small,
grown-up bass in my voice.

apparently alligators got nasty mouths too
and one of them must have
got slick and called Papa out his name
cause he came home and as Granny
told him the story he just nod his head,
pull the skin of that gator from
around his waist and cut both my cheeks
raw with a beating so good
that gator 'bout came back to life.

that was the last time Helen or Granny
had any troubles from my tongue,
and I ain't been that close
to a gator since.

Outfield Cot

Josh Gibson

sometimes when we on the road
and we need a place to stay
and just hop on the bus full of
everything we own and
ride till we stumble cross the nearest inn.

when we real lucky
the moon look like a pearl
before the first pitch
and the stars light up
just enough for innkeeps to see
all the black on our faces
that they don't want to rub off
on they pillow cases,
then pretend to read some sheet
that says they at capacity for the night.

round that time we all bob our heads
as if we understand what he mean
and walk real proud to the bus
to ride the few blocks down
the street to the park.

once we there we each find us a spot
somewhere in the outfield grass,
get real comfortable on our fresh-cut cot
and all my teammates count sheep.

I don't waste my time with that foolishness.
I like to lay back, like to count the stars,
see if I can't pick out the one
I'm about to hit next.

Worship

Josh Gibson

I get my church in on Saturday night
when the band plays some gospel
with all the soul
but none of the church hats
white gloves or begging for money.

we tithe on Saturday night.
that way we know where the money goes.
Jimmy behind the bar always get a good tip
whoever on the guitar guaranteed
first pick at whatever women left
who ain't trying to make it home tonight
after all the players get theirs,
and the spirits flow through that joint
so smooth it ain't nothing to see
some lace laying on the floor.

we don't need no preacher-man
to get us all sweaty, to empty
out our pockets, to help us catch
some far-off idol. we got us,
and love, and blues, all the same,
within the four corners of that juke.

and when Saturday night ain't enough,
once the band done packed up,
and everyone escort they lucky lady out,
we only got a few more hours, 'til baseball.

Trucutu

Hooks Tinker

> Babe Ruth was the white, left-handed Josh Gibson.
> —*Anonymous*

down in Trujillo
they got this comic strip
of a time-traveling caveman
named Trucutu that carries
a stone war *martillo*
spends his time in the jungle
fighting dinosaurs the size
of four or five elephants
and he only wears a loincloth
rides his pet Dinny
and his girlfriend Ooola
is always close by

when Josh emerges from the dugout,
you can hear fans in the stands
start to whisper in their seats
Trucutu, resending into a chant
as he carries his wooden mallet
and walks past the on deck circle
and marches into the jungle
to fight baseballs away
from the catcher's mitt

down in Trujillo
when they gave Josh a new name

they made sure to christen him
something more saintly
than any of the ones
they got up in the states

Perejil

Josh Gibson

Trujillo done rolled out the red carpet
for Negro Leaguers first chance he get,
which is something Roosevelt
ain't never do or done before.

he let us wear his name,
a big *Trujillo* cross our chest,
and pay us good money, fine
liquor, fair weather, and more
beautiful skirts than we can count.

I never been one to speak
that Dominican-type Spanish,
but seem Trujillo and his money
don't really mind. and seeing how
negro contracts don't get no gate
an opportunity to walk out
to leave behind that white mess
them americans worship so much
is like a psychic playing numbers.

rumor been that Gus don't like paying his players
but I ain't never had no problems with that.
only reason I took a trip down south is cause
Trujillo got them big bucks,
sugar and rum type money,
and baseball race-free down there.

but ain't that some type of nonsense?
Trujillo liking Negros, more than Roosevelt.

The Base Watch

Josh Gibson

when a black man think about stealing
the only thing that put the fear a god in him
more than the police is when he stand
twelve feet off first base and he know
I'm behind the plate.

he'll twitch, jump, flinch, grunt,
even take a jab step or two to try
and draw a throw or my attention.

what he don't know is I got the strength
of mind to see the future, to read his every
thought all the way down to which side
of the base he plan to grab or swipe.

you'd think by now they'd realize
this here arm is responsible for catching
a whole lotta would-be thieves and crooks
rounding them up like them mobs
of white preachers, policemen, shopkeepers
and sending them back to they jail cell of a dugout.

if a fan ever come to a game
and a man able to steal something from me
understand, that player must have caught
my shortstop or second basemen napping.
he most likely said a good prayer last night,
and no doubt tithed generously last Sunday.

Winter Ball

Josh Gibson

I.

Puerto Rican Women
are even sweeter than they look.

I mean there was this one
and I met her outside the locker room
and she handed me some Pitorro
and I whispered some phrase
in Spanish and I followed her round for
a whole week.

Then you got them women
down in Trujillo land
and every last one got these
half-dress half-skirts on
and there is this big parade
with drums and dancing
when we get there and this one
I always make sure to visit
when I come down and she
keeps a couple bottles
of Brugal waiting on the nightstand.

Then there's the way them
american Black Women

can ride the sounds of the horns
inside the Crawford Grill so clean
we can't tell whether each of us
still got on clothes and we all smell
of cocoa and sweaty liquor and that thing we do.

But back to Puerto Rico.
Can't nobody mess up some sheets
like them, turn around and make it look like
I was never there, swallow up every trace of evidence
and walk out the room looking better than they did before
I got my hands on them.

Their Baseball Fields are like their women's
freshly made beds to me. I see them more as
an empty canvas than as a bunch of grass and dirt
with a fence almost tall enough to block
the perfect row of palm trees about fifty feet behind.

When I'm down there, I like to plant as many baseballs
inside the branches of them palm
trees as I can, and listen to the way
it sounds when they try to keep count.

2.

I hope ghosts don't exist.
if so, I need them to stay put
in the place they last made love.
that way Helen never sees what I do.

3.

A suitcase can be as spacious
as them big plantations
in the South if you know
how to make it work.

By the time even the most jumbled
up ball player spend a year with the men,
he learn how to fit his whole life inside a bag.

Most of them young ones
spend they first season wishing
they could fit they wife inside.

I spent every night up late
wishing I could
and sometimes could not
forget all about mine.

4.

Time moves different for us.
we don't say bye when we go to work
we pretend we got two families
and they both know all about the other.

One gets us for holidays
birthdays
anniversaries.

The other gets us in between
road trips
barnstorming
pennant celebrations.

We all migrate
from the North to catch
some of the warmth down South
and always come back
a little bit darker each time.

BOTTOM OF THE SIXTH
3–2 CRAWFORDS

Resurrection

Josh Gibson

If Helen ever get another breath,
ever rise up out the ground,

I'll challenge god, pitcher vs. hitter,
my bat against his best stuff.

I'll tell him no cheating this time
no doctoring balls, and no early deaths.

Tell him his son can't umpire
nor none of his angels.

This heavyweight bout is on my terms,
and I doubt a single strike gets by me.

But *if* he catch me on my heels
put me a pitch away from death

I'll shorten my stroke, stay alive
until he makes a mistake.

Then, I'll hit that ball so fast
only thing he catch is whiplash.

While he search all them stars he created
for the one I just hit, I'll sprint round them bases,

right on past home, hold Helen by the hand,
find the twins, and introduce them to they mom.

The Magician

Josh Jr.

all my friends think since I got the best
Negro League stars as uncles,
games of pickup baseball
on the block more fun if I'm on they team.

I almost only see my pretend uncles
when they come by Granny's House
with Papa whenever he in town
from some barnstorming
or a trip down in the Islands.

he like to bring the best ones
all my friends' favorites—
Satch, Cool Papa Bell, Judy Johnson.
the players whose stance or delivery
on the field my friends spend hours
in front of their mommas'
mirrors trying to imitate.

after a few visits each *hey*
the players toss out with quarters for candy
starts to wear off, and my friends see
each one of my play uncles
ain't no more or less man
than they daddies or granddaddies.

there is this one player named Sammy
who become a slight exception.
I can't figure out how, but the more
Papa show up with Sammy
the slower his speech get
and the more he smell like
he done emptied a few hundred bottles,
mixed in with the scent
of a skunk-covered pine tree.

every time Papa come round
with Sammy they always real happy
but it ain't got nothing to do with us,
with they chance to see me or Helen.

it's like they got they own world
with its own language and jokes
that can't none of us make out.

where Sammy a conjure man
who so good at his newest trick
I can stare into the eyes of my father
and still never see him.

Battle of the Greatest

Satchel Paige

> I'm not gonna throw smoke at yo' yolk.
> I'm gonna throw a pea at yo' knee.
> —*Satchel Paige*

Gibson been blessed three times.

first, for coming out of his mother's
womb black as a storm. Second,
for being able to hold all that thunder
and lightning inside a bat. Third, of course,
for getting to step into the box and face me.

people say Satch vs. Josh
was like the battle
of the titans and the gods,
like Shango vs. a Mopane Tree,
or David vs. Goliath.

but in this story, the giant and David
stood on the mound together, one
stretching to the Heavens while the other
slung enough baseballs to intentionally walk
the bases loaded for Josh, and his dull
one-sided wooden axe, to try and keep me
from playing catch with Campy.

I told Josh what was coming. aimed
for the blackness of Campy's mitt
threw three balls past the storm
and watched them all disappear.

later that night, I let good ol' Joshua know
his only problem was that I'm too good.

I did leave him with some advice. I suggested
in the future, when he finds himself on his knees
talking to his Creator, he might want to ask for something
to be done about that hole in his bat.

Late-Night Ritual

Josh Gibson

before each plate appearance I grab
the only bat ain't been worn out yet,
rest it on my shoulder real mellow,
since the hits come from how you treat them.

I pause at the top step, let the fans breathe
life into my every stride to the on-deck circle,
I inhale each whisper and send its energy
down to my forearms, and store it there.

since ain't no time for foreplay once I'm in the box,
I take my time studying the pitcher's every act.
all I need is one pitch to know everything down
to the last time he washed his jockeys.

now I ain't the first player built with a solid frame.
but even then, can't no one touch a ball like me.

I tell some it's all about how I study the game,
slow it down so that every lace look like a bullseye,
pick up every little hint the pitcher might give off on accident.

but the secret, the real magic
happens at night,
when everyone is gone home
I spend however long is needed rubbing
my hands over the barrel of my bat
like I did Helen's back before we slept
to make sure she stays smooth.

and the real secret be when it's just the two of us,
I pour some rum I brought back
onto the floor whisper an apology
for hitting the ball so hard
and take a big, long sip.

The Bats Speak

Josh's hands be the opposite
of the teeth that saw had when
it cut me too small to grow anymore.

Gentle Josh grasp my neck, lift me
off the ground, slide his palms
down my waist and hold firm
before we go to war.

When he swing me through the air,
it ain't as violent as people think.
the way he place me on his shoulders,
hold me close enough to blend bronze
fingers with hickory skin, I have come
to quite like. every time we meet, he
loads his hips back slightly, takes in a full
lungs' worth of air as the pitch is being delivered
and throws all we got toward center field.

For us, love is rough: cruel.
And this power, this dominance,
feels too good: making
everything white submit.

When we finish up with our little dance
he likes to toss me off to the side
so he can take a quick lap around the bases.

And a small part of me is waiting
for the first time he considers
I might want to join him in his trot.

Deep Breath

Josh Gibson

only thing more holy
than that scent
of fresh ash or maple
is when some piece of Helen
been left behind
and brush up against
one of my senses.

how a few of her hairs,
her favorite bottle a lotion,
our pillows, nail polish,
the twins remind me
she ain't gone
but ain't really here, either.

in the morning
I liked to rest my chin
on top of her head,
right before I left the house
to race the sun to the mill,
I'd draw in this breath
that make you think
I was 'bout to be thrown over
the side of some ship.

I'd force all that air to carry me
the whole way to work. I kept a list
in my head of each special scent

I could name. Like how her breath
only half stink in the morning.
how her skin never quite shake the smell
of every ounce of the love we done made.

last night both the children was on they knees
at the foot of Helen's bed. Together, they pretend
they could whisper to the dead and somehow
they hushed prayers silenced the creak
that one floorboard make to remind me how big I am.

right before they told her goodnight
they said they worry something wrong
cause I move too slow, they say it's almost
like I got bad knees, whenever I come around
Helen's Mama's house.

I still ain't gained the strength to tell them
how hard it is to move fast
when I still ain't found a way to exhale

BOTTOM OF THE NINTH
3–2 CRAWFORDS

Living Will

Josh Gibson

When I'm gone, tell all the little boys
and girls never to confuse a baseball cutting
through the night sky with a shooting star.

Let them know that not all my home runs
were launched to the corners of the universe.

When my heart stops beating
the game of baseball stays.

Don't empty no bottle, even
if it's the smoothest liquor
you find, over my grave.

I want to rest somewhere that looks like
the mix of infield dirt and grass,
place home plate aboveground at my feet,
let my body rest under the right-handed batter's box
build the fence at least four hundred feet away
and open a hotdog stand close enough
for the smell to warm up my bones.

Every Sunday I want the beautiful black woman
who looked a lot like Helen would have
with the perfectly sewn hats, who always sat
three rows up, dead center, behind first-base dugout,
to wave at me as she walks down the street to the field.

Don't write nothing fancy on my headstone.

Bury me with my bat,
somewhere close to my wife,
and give my children a kiss.

Youth Fountain

From Satchel Paige's Six Rules for Staying Young

every time your cleats
are laced up, remember winning
the series might mean losing game one,
then make sure your broom is right close,

but don't you ever angry up
your blood, it's red not black,
it don't like them fried foods,
the mind speaks to the stomach
control both,

I call the pitches.

don't you ever shake me off,
don't drop a strike, or a ball,
matter fact,

inside of you there are spirits that hold
more power than a packed house
and it's your job to keep them
flowing by jangling around gently as you move,
don't do no nonsense, no mess,
be proud
go very light on the vices,
you know like
carrying on in society, the social ramble ain't restful,
never run, ever, under any circumstances,
by no means should you ever
look back,

something might be gaining on you,
just be here

and never forget to be young.

My First Slump

Josh Gibson

when I get a new bat
I like to check for splinters
rub off any dust, see to it the curves
are perfect. I like to place my nose
where the grain splits and smell
an entire forest of trees
sacrificing theyself to one day
maybe find they way into my hands.

I done picked up all types of bats
maple, hickory, ash but none of them
like my first one.

I never been known to break a bat,
but I do make sure to wear them
out before I send them to retirement.

the first one was different.

named it after her and
she never got wore out
never broke,
never chipped or splintered.

she just reach down inside herself
find me a couple home runs
until one day, for some reason,
she went to sleep.

Mama and Her Daughter

Helen Gibson Jr.

There is this lady who walks with her daughter
every Saturday round one in the afternoon
and the two of them got maybe
enough space between them
to fit a little baby doll or half a bag of groceries
and they don't really say nothing to one another
but you can tell they mother and daughter
cause they look just alike
and like I said they don't never really speak
to each other on their walk
and I can't never tell where 'xactly they going
but I imagine it's somewhere important
and I never done gathered the courage
to follow them around the corner to see
where they headed but I always make it a point
to press my nose up against the glass
and just look and I never spend the energy
to try to hide it neither and I know you probably think
I don't hide cause I want to be found out
but truth is I don't care
one way or the other
I just find it fascinating you know
how this mother and daughter can walk down the street
so close every Saturday and sync up everything
like I can tell this little girl who must be
six or seven or eight she must have spent the first
three four or five years of her life just following
her mother around learning how to walk

how to flow through space with each stride
so that she draw just enough attention
to get folk to look but also in that look understand
how much respect she owed
and the two of them walk down the street
Mama got this dress on
it's got these bright white buttons down the front
and the shoulders real broad
like she done smuggled some goddess up in there
and she always got a different bag in her hand
and today it was this deep red
with some sparkly stuff on it and these heels
that I can't see how she could glide in them like that
and they always always match the bag
and right next to her was her daughter
who had on some slim dress
that was oftentimes white
and it almost always have some form of polka-dot pattern
and them dots would match the heels and the bag
and Mama must be able to sing
cause I know that she humming some tune cause
they strides was just, perfect, like they was marching
but something more rhythmic
and whenever they come round
no one ever on the street
and it be like the sidewalk
want to turn gold
I never seen it
but I can feel it.

and today
Jr. come up right behind me
and he ask me what I'm looking so hard at

and without taking my eyes off them
I point and say Mama and her daughter
and usually Jr. be outside this time of day
but it rained and there was this little pocket
protecting the two of them from a single drop
of what Granny call the Angel's tears
and he got the mind to pretend they ain't there.

Let Us Be

Josh Gibson

Sammy got this game we play
where we move the kitchen table
out the way when his lady sneaks
upstairs to sleep. we stack bottles
tall enough to block the light
from the lamp hanging
over the empty spot
where we all ate dinner
to see which of us can last longer.

his wife's named Helen too.
she serves as our judge
when she comes downstairs
for her morning coffee
and clanks a few empty
bottles together
as an alarm clock
sounding like the bell
before a round of boxing
so we hop up off the canvas
and look for her to declare a winner.

she real good at cleaning up our mess.

some mornings we make the team decide
which of us get to wear the heavyweight
belt cause his Helen never tells us who won.

these bouts in the locker room
are the best. we get to sleep
on the floor when we get a game going
and we always real neat with our pyramid.

sometimes we play a version of this game
with women when we on the road
and stack they bodies almost level
with our highest-reaching mountain of bottles
and since this version of the game got the same name
we both got us a good alibi.

Home Run #800 and Something

I feel stronger now
cause I got much less
control over how far
these home runs go

and it's got me wondering
what is on the other side of Heaven
back behind that edge
that no one ever gets to see
I mean it can't go on forever
can't be endless cause if that was true
I'd be able to get there too
and if he fair and righteous
he'd at least let me come visit

Maybe I can't seem to hear you anymore
because on the other side of Heaven
back behind the throne
is all the dark stuff that he don't want no one to see
and back there I just know he got you chained up

and I can feel him shaking
cause he knows I'm coming
and I'm bringing my bat

EXTRA INNINGS

Cooperstown

Hooks Tinker

everything about baseball white
but it's the Negro that make it a game.

I've seen more out of
our version of play
in a single nine innings
than a whole season of theirs.

baseball,
and this country,
already missed they chance
to make all this mess right.

they should have never
been afraid of they mediocrity,
never feared being shown up.

if there is one example
sufficient to knock out
all they nonsense
about they superiority
it's that time Josh flattened a fastball
from they league's so-called MVP, Dizzy Dean.

Josh hit that ball so hard, Dean
took himself out the game.

this is how we know
every record they hold
before integration
is a lie.

now, it does feel good
to see Josh's face
mixed in with all them greats
bronze profiles making them seem
immortal to all the living.

but what I want to see,
what Josh would have loved,
is when you hang up our portraits,
salute all our genius
and power, all our finesse
and flair, praise every drop
of beauty, let all your fear go.

Then, and only then,
do I give you the right
to say *play ball.*

Where We Go

Helen Gibson

The cruelest part about this afterlife
is being outside of time to see in this form
that I am everywhere for you and not nearly
close enough in the same moment

For me, I know all that will and has yet
to happen for you, that these words
are no comfort and worse,
you will never read them
in your life, and this is almost too much

Here, my second favorite pastime
is to visit that one night, cold, snow suffocating
every inch of outside, and you and I
made ourselves warm and the two of us
laid there and said our vows for the first time

For me, that is now.
For you, a painful past that no human
should ever have to bear alone

And I wish that there was some god
here in this place that I could plead with
because that would mean that somewhere
we would be in some old rocking chairs
on the front porch of some decent house
you'd be just into retirement from baseball
with big rooms for a bunch of us to dance

and it wouldn't be like none of those parties
your mother throws that I know you hate so much

And this is where I always make up this memory
of the instant you get here and I show you
how to move through time and space all over again
and suggest that we go to that one moment
and you smile, and we never come back.

The Walk Off

or "I Visit Josh's Grave"

Get up Josh
You ain't no Lazarus
You don't need Jesus
No god
You just you
Here is a bat
Get up
Get up
Get up Josh
I brought you a glove
Let's play catch
I ain't much on pitching
But we can hit if you just get up
They let us play now
You hear
They let us play
And they say you was the greatest
You hear me
The greatest there ever was
And I just wanna see
Can I see
Can you get up
It's me
I'm just a fan
My name is Dorian
I got power
But not like you and
I read about you once

My high school librarian
Found the only book in the whole school
That mentioned your name
And my English teacher told me to write about you
And I brought some poems for you
If you want to listen
That's cool
But I just wanna play
Can we play
I know it's weird
Me standing over your grave and such
But I think it's weird you're pretending to sleep
So please just
Get up
They let us play now
They even said sorry
Let you in the Hall of Fame
Gave you your record
That I know you already had
Maybe one day name the award after you
But they say it's better now
They ain't lynching us no more
They don't kill us as much
And we can work for them
For more money now
And it's cool
And we done rewrote the record books
And we didn't even have you
But you gotta get up to see
You gotta get up
Get up Josh
I'm putting together a team
You were my first pick
But you gotta get up

Please
I know you ain't Lazarus
And Jesus ain't done much for us
So I figured I just ask you
Straight
Get up
I even got you a uniform if you just rise up
I wanna see
I wanna see what they kept me from
I wanna see what they was so afraid of
Get up Josh
Get up
You can't die
Please

Just get up

ACKNOWLEDGMENTS

First, Mom and Dad, you saw this book, these poems, and most importantly this poet long before I did. You watered the soil around me, ensured I had enough room to grow, and have kept me well nourished with love. The best teammate and opponent I have ever had, Devin—all these years, and we still haven't taken a loss. My wife, Reecie, has supported me, these poems, and this family with unyielding dedication. My two children, Amiri and Damian, have been my motivation to complete this project; your presence in this process has helped me appreciate all the joy you bring. Frank X Walker, since that day you visited the library of Tates Creek High School, your mentorship-turned-friendship has been invaluable, and may this be only my first book to share the shelves with yours. Phyllis Schlich, about five feet from the doorway to your classroom, you ignited this project with a simple question, and each poem after thanks you.

I have been blessed with far too many great teachers to name you all, but to all, I am grateful. To Jennifer Eldridge and Lauren Nunemaker, I walked into the library looking for a book, and because of your help, next time, I'll walk in holding this one. Dr. Rynetta Davis, you introduced me to so many of the authors who now live in my head. Also, I hope you can forgive me for taking every single class you taught at the University of Kentucky. Angel C. Dye and Tiara Brown, thank you for poring over early versions of these poems in poetry workshops, and more importantly, for friendship. Angel Clark, you have helped me see poems live all around. Yvonne Johnson, a poem ain't a poem until you say so. Jeremy Paden, I hope these poems are as good as your cooking. To the Affrilachian Poets: being in this family, receiving your love and support, is a gift I hope I return in all that I do.

I started this project as a baseball player. More specifically, as a Black baseball player committed as a preferred walk-on to the University of Kentucky baseball team. I finished this project as a high school English teacher with a wife and two kids. When I penned this collection's first poem, it was in an independent study to fulfill the requirements to remain eligible for baseball and to graduate. Josh and his story have helped me appreciate my time in the game and more importantly those whom I love most after my playing days were done. This country, Major League Baseball, and life were cruel to Josh and his family. I want to leave this last space to acknowledge all those who spend their time bearing witness to his life, aim to right the wrongs of the past, and love deeply.

"Manifesto for Black Baseball Players" first appeared in *Black Bone: 25 Years of the Affrilachian Poets,* edited by Bianca Lynne Spriggs and Jeremy Paden (Lexington: University Press of Kentucky, 2018), 132–33.

Earlier versions of "My First Bat" and "West Field"—titled "Home Run" and "Escape"—appeared in *Shale Undergraduate Arts Journal,* University of Kentucky, fall 2014 (pages 16 and 86); many thanks to the editor, Katie Cross, for publishing the first of these poems.

At last, a wish: that the Major League Baseball's MVP award be renamed in Josh's honor.

Made in the USA
Las Vegas, NV
12 January 2024